This Book was created to help little ones connect with God's Word in a joyful and engaging way. Each page features a simple, uplifting Bible verse alongside a fun illustration to color...perfect for quiet time, Sunday school, or family activities. This book is designed to encourage meaningful conversations, spark faith, and create long lasting memories as parents and kids enjoy coloring together.

Enjoy!

The Lord is good to all.

PSALM 145:9

WITH GOD ALL THINGS ARE POSSIBLE.

MATTHEW 19:26

OBEY YOUR PARENTS IN THE LORD.
EPHESIANS 6:1

THE JOY OF THE LORD IS MY STRENGTH

NEHEMIAH 8:10

THE EARTH IS THE LORD'S, AND EVERYTHING IN IT.

PSALM 24:1

WHEN I AM AFRAID, I WILL TRUST IN YOU.
PSALM 56:3

JESUS CHRIST IS THE SAME

YESTERDAY, TODAY AND FOREVER
Hebrews 13:8

SING
TO THE LORD
A NEW SONG

Psalm 96:1

THE LORD GIVES STRENGTH TO HIS PEOPLE

PSALM 29:11

AS FOR ME AND MY HOUSE, WE WILL SERVE THE LORD

Joshua 24:15

BE STILL, AND KNOW THAT I AM GOD

PSALM 46:10

THE LORD IS FAITHFUL TO ALL HIS PROMISES

PSALM 145:13

IF ANY OF YOU LACKS WISDOM, ASK GOD.
JAMES 1:5

FOR GOD SO LOVED THE WORLD

JOHN 3:16

LOVE ONE ANOTHER.
-JOHN 13:34

DO NOT BE AFRAID, FOR I AM WITH YOU.
- ISAIAH 41:10

CHILDREN ARE A GIFT FROM THE LORD:
-PSALM 127:3

TRUST IN THE LORD WITH ALL YOUR HEART.
PROVERBS 3:5

GOD MADE THE ANIMALS.
GENESIS 125

YOU ARE LIGHT OF THE WORLD.
MATTHEW 5:14

PEACE I GIVE YOU.

JOHN 14:27

THE LORD IS MY SHEPHERD.
PSALM 23:1

REJOICE IN
THE LORD ALWAYS.
PHILIPPIANS 4:4

BE STRONG AND COURAGEOUS.

-JOSHUA 1:9

SERVE THE LORD
WITH GLADNESS.
- PSALM 100:2

LOVE YOUR NEIGHBOR AS YOURSELF.

- Mark 12:31

SHOUT FOR JOY TO THE LORD PSALM 100:1

HONOR YOUR FATHER AND MOTHER

EXODUS 20.12

DO GOOD,
SEEK PEACE.
PSALM 34:14

TEACH ME YOUR WAYS, LORD. PSALM 86:11

WE LOVE BECAUSE HE FIRST LOVED US

1 JOHN 4:19

GOD WILL HELP YOU

ISAIAH 41:13

EVERY GOOD GIFT
IS FROM ABOVE
JAMES 1:17